NINA CAMPBELL
INTERIOR DECORATION

NINA CAMPBELL
INTERIOR DECORATION
ELEGANCE AND EASE

Nina Campbell

Giles Kime

Foreword by Carolina Herrera
Principal photography by Paul Raeside

RIZZOLI
NEW YORK

New York · Paris · London · Milan

CONTENTS

FOREWORD

The originality of Nina Campbell's style is due to the fact that her rooms never look decorated.

She imbues her rooms with a feeling that seems always to have been present. Nina doesn't follow fads or fashion; in her own quiet way, she creates them. Her revolutionary ideas stem from good English tradition, with an eye for comfort and a wonderful sense of the curious.

I imagine the jolt of excitement that first-time visitors to Annabel's must have felt when they descended to the world's most glamorous basement. With its mixture of whimsy, comfort, and taste, they couldn't have been anywhere but in London in a club owned by the late, great Mark Birley, her creative co-conspirator. I feel the same excitement whenever I see Nina's work, whether it was created in the 1960s or today—her design is ever evolving, never still.

Over the years, the principles of Nina's art remain the same—color, comfort, harmony, and the bravery to sometimes step out of line. This magical combination ensures that Nina's work will never fail either to delight or to surprise.

—Carolina Herrera
New York, New York

INTRODUCTION

The London design world was a very different place when Nina Campbell started work at Colefax and Fowler in 1964, at just nineteen years old. There was no internet, no email, and no AutoCAD to turn the one dimensional into three-dimensional renderings. Nor was there the almost infinite choice of off-the-peg options that dazzle today's interior designer.

Economically, London was different, too; patronage was still firmly in the hands of the landed, rather than the new generation of homeowners whose wealth is in finance, energy, and technology. Clients were also predominantly British rather than international. Interior design was a more hands-on business. A limited range of choices meant that most elements of a scheme were bespoke; paint colors, textiles, trimmings, and furniture were the result of a detailed brief given by a designer to an artisan. The generation of designers schooled in this art have an advantage; commissioning requires the confidence borne out of skill and knowledge. It also requires clear and precise communication. The results are different too; it means that a room will be distinctive and fit a client like a glove.

One of the reasons that so many designers are drawn to the work of Nancy Lancaster and John Fowler, the two giants of interior design in the mid-twentieth century, is that their work—deeply steeped in the bespoke tradition of English design—has an effortless look that can only be achieved through obsessive attention to detail. Such a practice allows a designer's style to evolve because he or she isn't constrained by what is available—but by what, in his or her mind, is possible. It allows a designer to constantly develop new ideas and to turn them into reality. Nina's roots in the bespoke tradition are the key to her slow evolution from teenage apprentice to one of the most influential forces in interior design today.

This book allows the reader to chart that evolution of Nina Campbell's work, from the almost unhinged eclecticism in the 1960s when working with Mark Birley on the interiors of Annabel's through her own distinctive take on English Country

House style in the 1980s and 1990s to the pared-back—and very comfortable—classicism of her current work.

In the course of Nina's fifty-year career, British interior design has grown from a business that was little more than a cottage industry servicing the aristocracy to one that is truly global in its outlook. Today, Nina's clients are spread far and wide—in particular, in London, New York, Maine, and the Middle East. This is a testament not only to her ability to adapt her work to a broad range of different settings but also to the enduring appeal of classic English style.

British interior designers' engagement across a wide range of different territories has had an exciting impact on their work. It has encouraged them to absorb the influences of other cultures and to reflect them in their designs. Nina's body of work demonstrates this perfectly, from the influence of crisp, chic Manhattan decorating to Roman grandeur.

As well as embracing influences, Nina has also had an influence that reaches far beyond her own projects. Through her collections of fabrics and wallpapers, her books, and her witty and informative lectures, she has persuaded a whole generation that traditional style doesn't need to be either formal or stuffy.

It is also thanks to her that, over the last fifty years, the bespoke approach to interior design has come full circle; at the most elevated level, it is now hard to recognize patterns and colors that are standard issue. In the same way that everything in one of Britain's great eighteenth-century country houses was unique, so the most luxurious twenty-first-century interiors are the product of the skilled hand rather than the production line.

However, Nina's greatest contribution by far is her championing of the idea that the relationship between interior designer and client should be highly collaborative. This has put the client back at the center of the project; her focus isn't simply about the grand stylistic gesture but creating homes that reflect the tastes of their owners and understanding how her clients choose to live. No one could ever feel overwhelmed in a room designed by Nina Campbell—just cosseted and, more importantly, understood.

RECENT PROJECTS

Nina's recent work is the culmination of five decades in the field of interior design that started in the 1960s when she worked for Colefax and Fowler and then with Mark Birley, two of the most formative influences of her career. Her interiors have evolved—to reflect her own changing tastes and the eras in which she lived. While Nina has always been versatile in her approach, the breadth of work in the last decade demonstrates that she has the capacity to respond to almost any challenge, from large-scale projects in Belgravia and Jordan to historic buildings in Beverly Hills and Germany that require a light touch to bring them to life. This recent work is also the most timeless—a refined classicism and a growing modernist sensibility have combined to create interiors that are as relevant today as they will be in fifty years' time.

NEW YORK

Nina's most recently completed project in the United States—a collaboration with New York–based architecture firm Ferguson & Shamamian—is an apartment perched high above Manhattan. Stylistic breadth allows her to create interiors that reflect both the surroundings and the personalities of her many clients, whether located in London, Rome, New York, or elsewhere. For the owners of this cosmopolitan aerie, Nina has created environments in two locations, with startlingly different results. Yet, whatever the setting and style of a project, the DNA of Nina's work remains the same.

The dramatic color scheme and wallpaper that meet visitors in the entrance hall reflect the cosmopolitan feel of New York and create a cosseting mood, far removed from the freneticism of the city. Here, vitrines lined in flame-orange velvet and filled with flower pots—created by Tommy Mitchell in gold-and-white china—flank a terrace door (there is another version of this treatment, in her scheme for the Greystone Mansion in Beverly Hills, on page 158). Elsewhere in the apartment, the mood is more classic Nina, created by a combination of her own furniture designs and the recurring use of vibrant shades of blue. Paneling inlaid with chrome, a specially commissioned carpet in the study, and fitted cupboards in the bedroom add an extra dimension that couldn't be further removed from standard-issue Manhattan apartment block. The client's one directive—that each element should conjure happiness—has surely been achieved.

The woodwork in the entrance hall—lacquered by Dean Barger—is in shades of deep blue, and the walls are papered in Gondola by Cole & Son. The console is from KRB, a New York store where Nina gets many of the antique pieces for her projects in the United States. Scalamandré's Gran Condé Unito, a distressed silk velvet, in Spice covers the two chairs.

PRECEDING SPREAD AND
RIGHT: The inky blue of the
entrance hall appears again
in the living room's hand-
tufted rug by Tai Ping. The
walls are papered in
Travertine by Fromental; the
curtains are made from a
bespoke fabric by Vanners.
The sofa, designed by
William Switzer at Tatiana
Tafur, is upholstered in Silk
Puffs by J. Robert Scott.
The bench between the
display cases is upholstered
in Sora velvet by Kelly
Wearstler. FOLLOWING
SPREAD: Details from the
living room. The tables on
either side of the sofa are a
bespoke design by Nina, and
the screen is by de Gournay.

ABOVE: In the powder room, hand towels from Nina's own line are embroidered with silver dragonflies. The parrot sconces are from Baguès. OPPOSITE: The kitchen is by New York–based designer Christopher Peacock. Louvered shutters at the window are a practical choice for the confined space. The cabinetry and reverse-painted backsplash are in blue, which seamlessly continues the color of the adjoining entrance hall.

Fabric used for the blinds in the study is Tessa by Plumwich, the custom rug is from Pierre Frey, and the bespoke sofa is in Cantabria velvet by Nina Campbell (all of the designer's fabrics are available exclusively from Osborne & Little). The sofa table from Christopher Guy and the desk from Linley pair effortlessly with an antique chair.

PRECEDING SPREAD: The client's love of the color lavender has been interpreted in various materials in the master bedroom. The hand-painted, sheer silk at the window is from de Gournay, and the curtain tassel is from Spina. The three-legged table from KRB has a custom-colored lavender top. The mirrored bed is a bespoke design by Niermann Weeks, and the bedside table in shagreen is from Garrison Rousseau. ABOVE AND OPPOSITE: The guest bedroom wallpaper is Barrington by Nina. The Mabel chair, also by Nina, is covered in acid-green velvet.

ROME

I nterior design would be a simple business if it involved nothing more than reconfiguring and decorating a space. Instead, it has to meet the needs and expectations of a client—and in most cases, two.

The interiors of this elegant apartment on Rome's Via dei Condotti were commissioned by a couple with a wide range of interests and tastes. Thanks to a combination of furniture in simple shapes, a refined palette of bold colors, and striking contemporary touches, the result couldn't be further from a period piece. A layer of discreet sophistication has been added with a mix of decorative details: fabric walling edged with braid, deep fringes on the cloth covering the bedside table, and nailing that adds subtle definition to the sofa. Paneling and fitted joinery make the most of the space and help to manipulate proportions when required. In addition, robust structural elements such as the beamed-and-boarded ceilings and local influences such as colored cotto floors combine to create a style that imbues the apartment with a strong sense of place; no visitors could be under any illusion that they are anywhere other than this most ancient of cities.

The console table and mirror, both by London-based designer Birgit Israel, offer a contemporary take on a classic arrangement that epitomizes the careful balance of new and old, which Nina has achieved throughout this project. The pendant light by Delisle has a distinctly Roman feel.

PRECEDING SPREAD: The drawing room is dominated by a rich ruby red on a pair of the clients' own armchairs and the Travers braid that trims the fabric walling, which is from Lewis & Wood. ABOVE: A gilded armchair covered in Mart by Lelièvre is one of the many classic elements of the scheme. OPPOSITE: The dining area features the clients' extensive collection of works by eighteenth-century artist Giovanni Battista Piranesi.

The secret to the success of this project is the way that pared-back classic pieces are blended with designs that have a distinctly modernist feel. One example is the table and chair in the kitchen (above, left) from the Yacht collection by Soane Britain that is inspired by the furniture of 1930s ocean liners. The walls of the bathroom (above, right) have been transformed with mirror panels. The colored ceramic floor is an Italian specialty.

Ruby red is continued in the master bedroom, where a bedside table
covered in Carriage Cloth from Claremont has a deep Rouen fringe from
Samuel & Sons—the color is also used to trim the walls with Velvet Rings
braid from Travers. The linen-blend walling is Fortuna from Marvic.

The bathroom and dressing room have a distinctly masculine feel. The ceiling
light is from Charles Edwards, and the curtain fabric is Jaipur in red from
Titley and Marr. The open shelving helps to enhance the feeling of space.

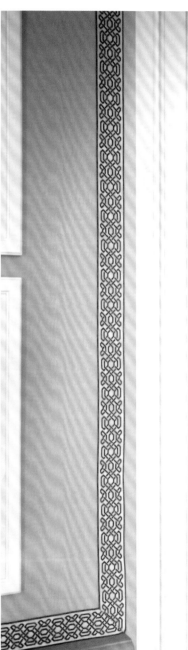
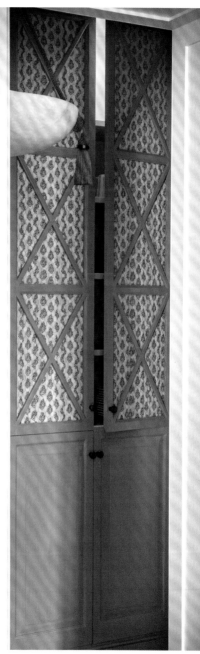

OPPOSITE AND ABOVE: One of the consistent themes in all of Nina's work is discreet storage that blends into the architecture of the space. Here, doors backed with Beleek by Titley and Marr, instead of being traditionally glazed, conceal closets that store china. FOLLOWING SPREAD: The relaxed family room is heralded by a change of color—Etro's Palinuro, a corduroy velvet in deep burnt orange, creates a warm, cosseting, more informal feel than the ruby red. The Halma Man Table is from Soane Britain and is finished in a custom lacquer.

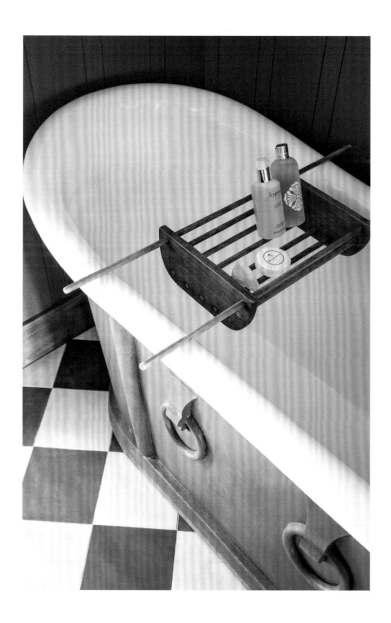

OPPOSITE: In the guest bedroom Nina has employed her technique of manipulating the proportions of a space with fitted joinery that reaches the height of the picture rail. A detail that is typical of Nina's work is a door that is incorporated into the joinery, creating a more coherent look. The headboard is a bespoke design from Nina Campbell Furniture that has been covered in Peter Fasano's Persia fabric. ABOVE: The adjoining bathroom is in a striking monochrome scheme.

In the children's bedroom, clever joinery makes the most of the space and
provides useful storage under the beds. Three Lotus lights from Gong,
suspended from the ceiling at different heights, illuminate the room. The walls
are decorated with a specially commissioned design by Marina De Lagarda.

LONDON

Fueled by both the Industrial Revolution and Britain's growing empire, London expanded in the nineteenth century. To the west it swallowed up villages such as Chelsea and Fulham, which had been bucolic market gardens in the previous century. Beyond the stucco-fronted houses of Belgravia are elegant redbrick terraces where many of Nina's clients have established themselves, conveniently close to Harrods, Brompton Oratory, and Hyde Park.

Leading from the front door, beyond a pair of curtains in deep blue velvet, guests are met with the sight of a fully fitted bar off to the left. The house was built in the period of William Morris and William De Morgan, when blues, ranging from cobalt to peacock hues, lent a glowing vibrancy to interiors. Throughout the house the color recurs on upholstery, blinds, paintwork, and trimmings—summoning up a feel that is distinctly nineteenth century. Yet there are modern touches, too—particularly in the garden designed by Stephen Woodhams, which provides the perfect setting for a sculpture by the husband-and-wife team François-Xavier and Claude Lalanne.

OPPOSITE: Italian strung curtains in Nina's Cantabria velvet create a buffer from the outside world as well as add a sense of drama. The trimmings on the curtains are from Samuel & Sons, and the horsehair in blue black on the stool is from John Boyd. The space has been opened up to create an inviting entrance hall. FOLLOWING PAGES: At the end of the entrance hall, a simple console has been created by covering a table in a fitted cover of Rubelli's Carlo in two shades: *Noce* and Denim. Parquet on the floor is left bare or covered with edged sisal carpets.

ABOVE: The bespoke bar, in a room that leads off the entrance hall, is complemented by a Regency sofa and a pair of antique lights from London dealer Carlton Davidson. OPPOSITE: The same room is lent an ethereal feel by London blinds in Maori fabric by Claremont. FOLLOWING TWO SPREADS: At the windows of the sitting room are curtains in Rubelli's Gianduja. The sofa is a bespoke design by Howard.

As in so many of Nina's schemes, the walls of the study are lined in fabric that not only absorbs sound but also creates a finish that is more robust than either paint or wallpaper. The sofa, from the historic chair manufacturer Howard, is covered in Nina's Fursdon. A tray of Italian glassware (above) sits on an ottoman in George Spencer's Wallace Stripe in aqua and red.

The centerpiece of the dining room is a magnificent table from the Parisian designer Philippe Hurel. The ceiling light was designed by Nina and made by the London bespoke lighting purveyor Dernier & Hamlyn in a Thai silk by Fox Linton. The walls are upholstered in San Marco by China Seas from Quadrille.

As with so many of Nina's projects, the key to this room is bespoke joinery such as the pair of mirrored cabinets that creates useful storage for formal china (above, left). The interior of the cutlery drawer (above, right) is painted in Orange Aurora by Little Greene, as are the cabinet interiors.

The cabinetry in the light-filled kitchen to the rear of the house is by Mark Wilkinson. The banquette creates space-efficient seating for the breakfast table. The pair of Thonet chairs in red creates a contemporary feel. The walls are painted in Little Greene's Clay Pale, and the kitchen cupboards are in Farrow & Ball's Dauphin.

The orangery-style kitchen offers views over the contemporary garden designed by Stephen Woodhams, who has created a number of different levels in order to lend a feeling of space. The garden is given a surrealist bent with a bronze apple by artist duo Les Lalanne.

ABOVE: Richly veined marble in the downstairs bathroom evokes a luxurious mood. OPPOSITE: In the
screening room, a wraparound sofa by Howard is upholstered in Silk Puffs in ivory that makes
the most of the available space. On the wall is Manila Hemp wallpaper in deep blue by Phillip Jeffries.
The Art Deco sconces, mounted on mirror panels, evoke the glamour of bygone cinema palaces.

As in other projects that Nina has worked on in towering London town houses, she was keen to avoid the potential monotony of a succession of stairs and landings. The stairs are carpeted in a bespoke runner from Pierre Frey, and the walls are painted in Clay Deep from Little Greene.

In the master bedroom, the mix of classic furniture in simple shapes and striking contemporary pieces such as the client's own floor lamp creates a look that is a perfect balance of traditional and contemporary. The embracing environment is enhanced by the wool curtains, with embroidered trim from Holland & Sherry.

OPPOSITE: Nina has created a discreet door that leads from the master bedroom to the bathroom, a feature that helps to simplify the space. The headboard is upholstered in Malmaison, from historic Venetian fabric house Fortuny. A damask-style fabric in chocolate brown covers the walls. ABOVE: The blinds fabric in the bathroom is Medara, in brown and navy on cream, from Home Couture.

The joy of fabric walls is that they offer the perfect means to address the challenge of awkward spaces such as attic rooms. In this top-floor guest room, the walls have been lined with Claremont's Alhambra in Rojo, which creates a warm, intimate feel that helps to soften the lines of the sloping ceiling.

KRONBERG IM TAUNUS

There are times when a designer's challenge is to revive rather than completely reinvent a space. Arguably, it's a greater feat than starting from scratch; styles and proportions created for another, very different era have to be embraced and made relevant to the modern world. One such project was Nina's commission to transform the interiors of the magnificent Schlosshotel Kronberg, which had been built in the 1890s as a Dower House for the Empress Friedrich (Princess Victoria, the eldest daughter of Queen Victoria). Inside and out, the style is an elegant expression of German Gothic Revival.

Nina was the perfect choice for the job; her deep understanding of the European decorative tradition and ability to create classic, comfortable spaces allowed her to pull the disparate elements together in one cohesive scheme. In places, the bold architectural features of the rooms have been softened with carefully designed curtain treatments and screens used to manipulate architectural proportions. The result is a feel that is true to the stately home's historic origins but unburdened by its history—or its extensive collections of work by Gainsborough, Rubens, and Titian.

The key to this project was to bring the space to life with inconspicuous touches that added both color and comfort. In the paneled library, Nina had the walls above the woodwork painted a striking blue, which serves as a magnificent backdrop for the paintings and porcelains. The bespoke carpet from Ulster adds a cohesive and decorative feel to the space.

In her design for the library, Nina employed an innate ability for creating arrangements of furniture that are complex but nevertheless coherent. The window blinds—in a moiré from Pierre Frey with applied stripes in Coromandel from Bennison—are sufficiently discreet to allow the Gothic Revival architecture of the schloss to speak for itself.

In the lobby, Nina worked with a combination of her own bespoke designs from her furniture line and existing items from the hotel. Here, items of her own occasional furniture perfectly complement a pair of back-to-back sofas in her Amisi fabric, which is finished with a deep bullion fringe (as seen on the following spread).

RIGHT: In this view of the lobby, chairs are upholstered in Nina's Beatrice fabric. With the exception of cushions in Etro's Arnica, all the fabrics are from her own collections. The walls are in Portland Stone Deep from Little Greene.
FOLLOWING SPREAD: This project employed Nina's impressive capacity to focus on the details required to create a bespoke feel that doesn't detract from the period atmosphere of a building.

The bedrooms on the upper floors required Nina's skill for creating a calm, cohesive feel from rooms with sloping walls and ceilings. Many items of occasional furniture are Nina's own designs such as the coffee table. All the upholstered pieces are covered in Nina's own fabric designs.

In the dining area of this suite's living
room, Little Greene's paint in Baked
Cherry creates a cosseting feel.
The project employed Nina's skill,
developed while working on period
London houses, for creating coherent
multifunctional spaces in confined spaces.

For the awkwardly shaped windows in this suite, Nina commissioned
fabric-covered shutters that are a more space-efficient alternative to curtains
and don't require rods or tracks. The panels and the headboard are
covered in Borderline's Ellie. The walls are in Nina's own Bicton stripe.

ABOVE AND OPPOSITE: Nina's Barrington wallpaper and fabric create a
delicate, feminine feel in this suite. The antique furniture in the bedrooms
is all from the collection of the client. FOLLOWING SPREAD: The decoration
of the suites demonstrated Nina's extraordinary versatility as a designer.

The dramatic character of
Bicton stripe by Nina
enhances the dramatic curve
of the wall. The fabric on seat
backs and cushions of the
pair of bergère chairs is
Antalya in red by Borderline.

WILTSHIRE

Architecture and interior design, in the right hands, can intersect with stunning results. The owners of this eighteenth-century farmhouse in Berkshire commissioned a glazed atrium that joined two parts of the house, creating a light-filled space that welcomes guests. Like any new-build space, it required warmth and texture that would act as a foil to new plaster and the clean lines of the columns and cornicing. This Nina delivered in the form of a few carefully chosen classic pieces—a Regency table, a Swedish bench, and a copper bath—that ensure that the room has as much charm and character as the rest of the house.

Elsewhere, the interiors are dominated by a mix of soft colors that are perfectly suited to the rural setting. The plaster walls of the large, formal drawing room are in a pale pink that falls short of sweetness, and the sofa is upholstered in a muted green velvet—underfoot a Scandinavian carpet draws these two hues together beautifully. Nina's approach to the bedrooms and bathrooms is typical of her ability to combine carefully planned, highly practical elements, including fitted joinery with pleasing touches such as the fabric-lined bed alcove that sits between the cupboards.

OPPOSITE: In this new addition to the house, Nina has employed a mixture of antiques, new decorative items such as the Oak Branch chandelier by Richard Taylor Designs, and an edged sisal rug to add character and texture to the crisp architecture of the space. FOLLOWING SPREAD: In the main sitting room, Farrow & Ball's Setting Plaster offers a soothing backdrop that is complemented by fabrics in similar hues. The sofa is in Cantabria, part of Nina's Bargello Velvets collection. The armchairs are in Oban, part of Nina's Brodie Weaves collection.

PRECEDING SPREAD: Paint & Paper Library's Stone IV lends a relaxed air to the garden hall. The Bridgewater sofa from Nina Campbell Furniture is upholstered in Crosslee, a design from Nina's Montacute Weaves collection. On the floor is a jute rug with leather binding. By the fireplace is a Bridgewater chair from Nina Campbell Furniture, also in Crosslee. OPPOSITE: A bespoke table by Jonathan Sainsbury provides a welcoming bar. The Melrose Swan Neck floor lamp is from Vaughan Designs, and the colored glassware is from Nina's shop on Walton Street. ABOVE: The shutters are covered in Nina's Portinari fabric.

The library has been given a distinctly Scottish feel with a tartan carpet by Stevens & Graham that is complemented with walls in Eating Room Red by Farrow & Ball. The Tennyson wing chair is from Nina Campbell's own collection of furniture, and the fender is from Acres Farm in Majilite faux leather from Dedar.

The dining area of the kitchen has blinds in Nina's own Fontibre design, which creates a relaxed, rustic feel. The table and chairs are from I & JL Brown, and the Cassis Leaf wall lights are from Vaughan Designs. The walls are in Aquamarine Deep by Little Greene.

In the kitchen a substantial island unit separates the area for food preparation from the dining space. Open shelving in the alcoves and the absence of wall-mounted cupboards create an open feel. The walls are in Stone I from Paint & Paper Library, and the cabinetry is in Hudson Bay from Crown Paints.

ABOVE: The window curtains on the upstairs landing are in Nina's Tabula fabric. A hallway runner, in shades to match the curtains, was made for the space by Roger Oates. The antique chest, used for storing linens, is surmounted by framed prints, sourced from an antiques fair by the designer. The Torosay wallpaper is Nina's design. OPPOSITE: The walls of the master bedroom are lined in cream linen. The bedspread is in Camille from Nina's Les Rêves collection.

A pair of fitted cupboards in the master bathroom offers plenty of storage space. The large chair is upholstered in cotton toweling, as is the cushion on the window seat, which adds luxurious comfort. The walls are in Salix from Little Greene, and the cupboards are in Stone I from Paint & Paper Library.

The wallpaper in this bedroom is Barbary from Nina's Fontibre collection. The Alice chair is from Nina Campbell Furniture, and the chest of drawers is from Chelsea Textiles. Nina found the pair of wicker-framed mirrors at Quindry and had a workaday bedside table painted acid green to add a note of spice.

This is a perfect example of joinery designed by
Nina blending effortlessly into a room. A niche
in the cupboard by the bed and a wall light remove
the need for a bedside table. The curtains are in
Le Castellet from Turnell & Gigon, and the walls
are in Stone I from Paint & Paper Library.

ASCOT

The boxes at Ascot Racecourse might offer a view over some of the racing world's most hallowed turf, but their style is functional. Inside, they offer the interior designer a blissfully blank canvas. Nina's client bought four centrally located boxes that were combined, as well as another box that offers easy access to the Winning Post Enclosure. Her brief was to create a stylishly comfortable environment for entertaining and relaxing between races.

In addition to some internal remodeling, the ceilings were lowered in places in order to discreetly accommodate services such as air conditioning. Nina's bold decorating scheme, which extends to the table settings, was based on an opulent combination of deep, rich burgundy and gold, echoing the owner's racing colors. Although the proportions are palatial by Ascot standards, she employed the same space-expanding tricks that she uses in the redecoration of confined London town houses and Manhattan apartments. One of these devices is a wall in the dining room that she covered from floor to ceiling in mirrored panels that reflect both the room and the racecourse beyond. Dining chairs designed by the Austrian architect Josef Hoffmann create a distinctly streamlined feel.

OPPOSITE: The view from the box over the course at Ascot—some of the racing world's most hallowed turf. FOLLOWING SPREAD: The dining table and console are from Davidson, and the walls are in Kintail by Nina Campbell. The carpet is from Simon Playle.

OPPOSITE: This corner of the room is dominated by a magnificent cabinet from Davidson. Next to the client's own chair is the Grace table from Nina Campbell Furniture. The walls are upholstered in Nina's Delamont fabric. ABOVE: Inset into the mirrored wall is a television screen, hidden behind an equestrian work of art, that allows guests to hear television commentary and watch close-up footage of the races. FOLLOWING PAGE: The sofa and chair by Tatiana Tafur are upholstered in Amersham from Colefax and Fowler, and the Pagoda coffee table is from Nina Campbell Furniture. The amber cut-glass lamp is from Lucy Cope. PAGE 129: Details of materials used in the viewing box—sumptuous fabrics and finishes in a masculine and calming palette.

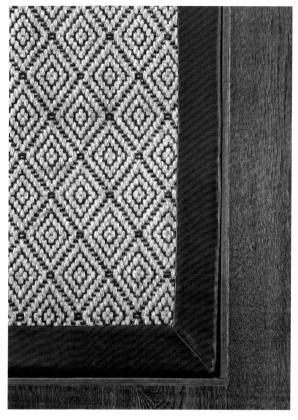

ABOVE: Nina created a space for top hats and umbrellas, stored between races. Cards identify names of hat owners. OPPOSITE: This luxurious area of the box has walls lined with Campbell Damask by Nina Campbell and is furnished with a Howard sofa covered in her Oban fabric. The bespoke armchair is made by Jonathan Sainsbury and upholstered in Sibton Straw by Claremont. The Charles X bucket chairs are from Soane Britain.

LONDON

When Thomas Cubitt laid out three garden squares in the early nineteenth century, one was named after Eaton Hall, the Cheshire home of the land's owner, the Duke of Westminster. Adjoining areas such as Eaton Place and Eaton Terrace also celebrated the Gothic Revival house designed by William Porden in 1820. Conversely, the style of Cubitt's buildings is resolutely neoclassical. Despite the huge amount of building in the surrounding area, Eaton Square, Eaton Place, and Eaton Terrace have remained virtually unchanged. For designers the challenge has been to bring them into the twenty-first century without diminishing their elegance.

This highly desirable part of London is one that Nina has known since childhood, and her understanding of the architecture was useful when she was commissioned to transform this house that was typical of the area. The brief for the project included a directive to incorporate a gym, a hair dressing salon, and a media room. These rooms were all accommodated below ground level and executed with the same simplicity and elegance as formal areas such as the drawing room—albeit in a more contemporary style. Upstairs, exquisite joinery combines with state-of-the-art technology to create a look and feel that offer the best of both old and new.

A decorative panel on the half landing, painted by Mark Done, disguises
a pair of doors. The carpet is a bespoke design from Braquenié, the
historic French company that dates back to the early nineteenth century.

PRECEDING SPREAD AND ABOVE: Original plasterwork ceilings were painstakingly restored and painted in a light, soothing color. The study is lent eighteenth-century glamour with a striking chimneypiece. The carpet was specially woven by Parsua to complement the colors of the one in the adjoining dining room. RIGHT: The lacquered walls of the dining room and antique sconces heighten the clubby feel. The back panel on the left disguises a jib door to the pantry. FOLLOWING SPREAD: The two distinct areas of the sitting room are furnished with Nina's Collingwood sofas in her Bovary fabric. The tables are from Taillardat. Braquinié custom wove the two carpets—the one in the front part of the room has more delicate roses, blues, and creams, while the other has bolder tones of the same colors.

ABOVE: On the garden terrace a table and chairs from McKinnon and Harris provide a comfortable setting for al fresco entertaining. OPPOSITE: A Regency chandelier from Vaughan Designs adds a stately mood to the library.

RIGHT: In the bedroom of the man of the house, the armchair from Nina Campbell Furniture is covered in Nina's Bovary in blue. The bed linens are from Monogrammed Linen Shop— renowned for its range of classic, luxurious linens and one of Nina's go-to sources. FOLLOWING SPREAD: Details from the gentleman's dressing room. The curtains are in a wool sateen from Holland & Sherry.

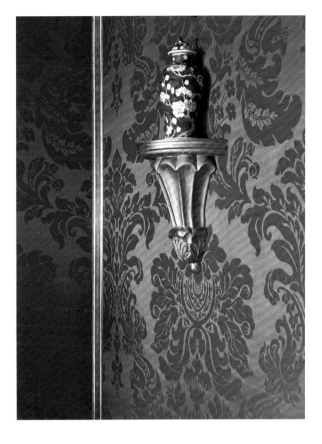

PRECEDING SPREAD: The bedroom of the lady of the house is a calm retreat with pale blue walls. Subtle glamour is added with bead trimming on the hangings of the half tester bed and an antique, mirrored dressing table. OPPOSITE: The adjoining bathroom is lent a crisp feel with Farrow & Ball's Cabbage White paint. The fittings are from Bathrooms International. ABOVE: The wallpaper in the dressing room is Nina's Folco pattern.

In the hallway, a floor-to-ceiling mirrored wall expands the sense of space. The console table is from the furniture and lighting specialist Porta Romana, the ceiling light is from Venetia Studium, and the wall lights are from Tyson Bennison.

ABOVE: The magnificent bed from Beaudesert in the guest suite, looking through to a white marble bathroom. The sheer bed hangings are in Nina's Woodsford fabric, which subtly contrasts with the pale blue wallpaper in the same Woodsford pattern. OPPOSITE: The basement includes a variety of amenities including a fully equipped hairdressing salon.

This "world within a world" includes not only a hairdressing salon and
a games room but also a steam room that is lined with mosaic tiles
from Sonite (above) and a mirror-lined gym by Technogym (opposite).

ABOVE AND OPPOSITE: The games room is dominated by a billiard table from Sir William Bentley Billards at one end and a pair of sofas from the Italian upholstery specialist Natuzzi at the other. The Mickey side table is from Nina Campbell Furniture. The walls are in suede-effect fabric from Stereo.

LOS ANGELES

The Tudor-inspired Greystone Mansion was designed by the architect Gordon Kaufmann and completed in 1928. The house, which is surrounded by formal English-style gardens, was built by oil magnate Edward Doheny as a gift for his son, Ned, and his family. Today the property is owned by the city of Beverly Hills and is widely used as a film location. In 2015, *Luxe Interiors + Design* magazine organized the Maison de Luxe Designer Showhouse and asked Nina to design a suite of rooms.

The result was a bedroom, bathroom, and massage room for a modern-day Edward Doheny, whose benevolent smile captured in a portrait imbues the bedroom with a genial mood. Nina was delighted to meet a member of the family who offered the portrait of her great-grandfather (the elder Doheny) to enhance the bedroom's décor. The room is rich with beautifully crafted architectural detail that Nina has brought to life with a paisley fabric on the walls and hangings on the four-poster bed, all in a sumptuous dark gray-green. A focus of the rooms is a collection of potted faux auriculas in metal created by Tommy Mitchell, displayed on wall brackets above the fireplace.

Metallic flowers in pots by Tommy Mitchell form a whimsical arrangement above the fireplace. The walls are in James Hare's Regal silk in Salix. The wall lights are from Collier Webb.

PRECEDING SPREAD AND RIGHT:
The bedroom walls are
upholstered in Nina's Khitan,
an opulent paisley damask
pattern. The satin bed
hangings are trimmed in braid
from Samuel & Sons, and
the bed linens are from
Leontine Linens. A portrait of
Edward Doheny, who gave the
Greystone Mansion to his son,
Ned, and his family, adds a
distinctive mood to the suite.

The room is furnished in a mix of antiques—including a desk, table lamps, and chest of drawers from Nelson Antiques—and new pieces such as Soane Britain's Klismos chair, based on an ancient Greek design. The tray (opposite) is a design by Rita Konig for The Lacquer Company. A thick, woven floor matting from Stark lends a relaxed atmosphere to the room.

This project involved
working with the lavish
architectural detailing of the
Doheny residence that, in
some rooms, needed little
enhancement other than
sympathetic touches such as
towels and items of
upholstery, shown here in
the bathroom that was
part of the suite of rooms
that Nina decorated.

The walls of the massage room are in Nina's Mallory pattern, the chair and mirror are from Oomph, and the trolley is from Soane Britain. The blinds are in Bicton stripe, and the turquoise lamp is from Christopher Spitzmiller. All elements combine to form a tailored and relaxing space.

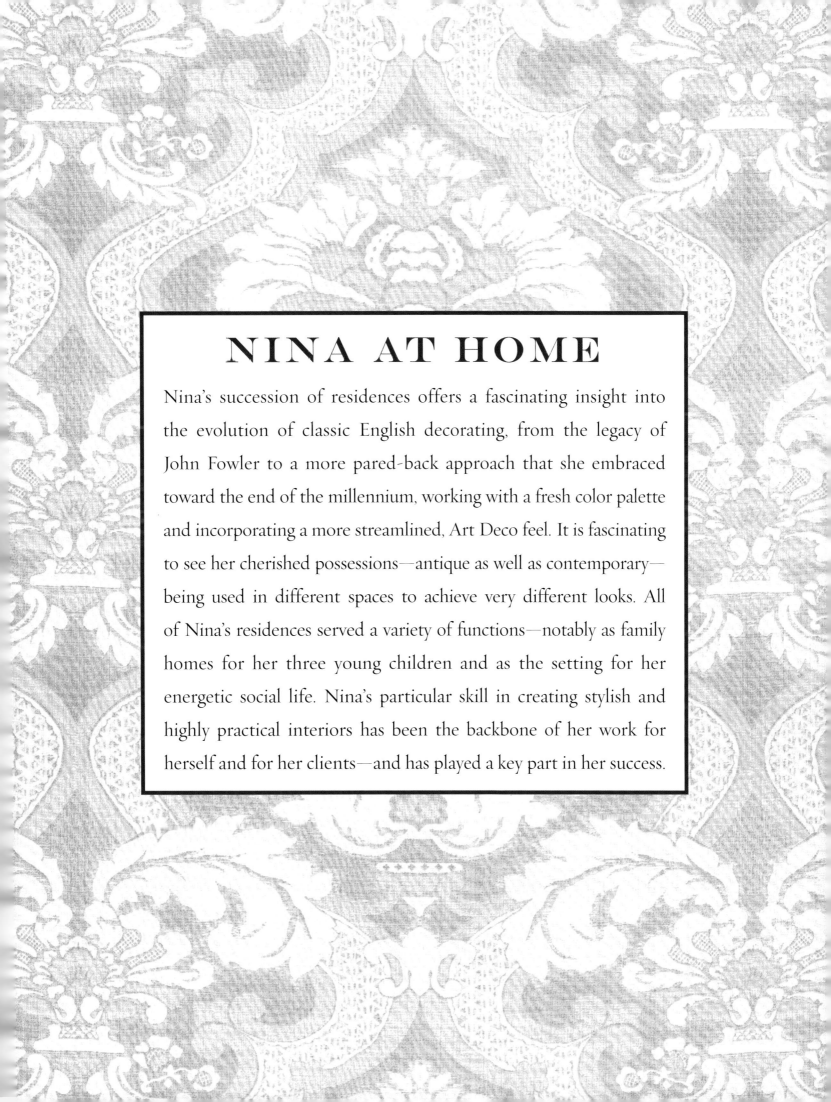

NINA AT HOME

Nina's succession of residences offers a fascinating insight into the evolution of classic English decorating, from the legacy of John Fowler to a more pared-back approach that she embraced toward the end of the millennium, working with a fresh color palette and incorporating a more streamlined, Art Deco feel. It is fascinating to see her cherished possessions—antique as well as contemporary— being used in different spaces to achieve very different looks. All of Nina's residences served a variety of functions—notably as family homes for her three young children and as the setting for her energetic social life. Nina's particular skill in creating stylish and highly practical interiors has been the backbone of her work for herself and for her clients—and has played a key part in her success.

LONDON
FULHAM

One of the many charms of Chelsea is its delicious mix of architectural styles that range from the splendor of Sir Christopher Wren's Royal Hospital to the Victorian grandeur of Cadogan Square. The neighborhood was famous in the seventeenth and eighteenth centuries for the production of both silk and ceramics. As London expanded in the nineteenth century, it became one of Chelsea's most prestigious districts. Today much of its charm lies in the fact that it comprises a number of distinct areas, each with its own character.

Off the western extreme of the King's Road (created for Charles II to make his way to Kew) is a grid of elegant Victorian houses with a combination of light and height that offered Nina the scope to create the feel of a country house with wide, exposed floorboards, high doorways, and grand nineteenth-century furniture. As ever, she reworked the downstairs to improve the flow, including the removal of a wall to create a dramatic dining space dominated by decorative panels. Upstairs the feel is similarly stately, with elaborate curtains in the bedroom. Compared to her previous homes in the area, the feel is slightly simpler, the beginning of a gradual shift in Nina's ever-evolving style to a more pared-back look.

The ceiling heights encouraged Nina to create a look that was more akin to a large English country house than a London town house; early nineteenth-century furniture, exposed wooden floors, and elaborate curtain treatments combine to create a look that is grand without being overbearing. Here the use of fabrics and wallpaper in a muted color palette creates a light, easygoing look that is more associated with the modern era.

In the drawing room Nina illustrates the great possibilities of fabric-lined walls, a common feature of her interiors. Fabric wallcovering is robust, offers insulation, and absorbs sound from both inside and outside a house. Thick, decorative cord creates a neat finish.

In the sitting room Nina employs symmetry to create a coherent feel in a space that comprises a variety of disparate elements. Matching pier glasses and floral arrangements on either side of the chimneybreast create the basis of the scheme. The club fender not only acts as a fireguard but also provides extra seating when entertaining large numbers.

A series of decorative panels creates a striking feature in the dining room downstairs, which is painted a deep red to create an intimate atmosphere. Other elements, including the striped upholstery and purple glassware, combine for an overall look that is striking and cohesive.

In the bedroom, Nina's Asticou toile in Coral creates a warm, decorative backdrop. At the windows, curtains and gathered pelmets are trimmed in fringing that lends the tailored scheme a bit of whimsy. Nina's mother's Spanish shawl is used as a bed covering.

ABOVE: In the bathroom, the fireplace, framed photographs, and a selection of antique furniture give the space a feel that is more akin to a living room. OPPOSITE: Wall lights, furniture, and works of art are displayed in a calming, symmetrical arrangement in the bedroom.

LONDON
NOTTING HILL

In 2002 Nina strayed from the more familiar territory of Belgravia and South Kensington to Notting Hill. While it is in the same borough, Notting Hill has a different feel, with shops and restaurants aimed at a younger crowd and good access to Hyde Park and Holland Park. She bought an apartment for herself, which comprised in essence two twenty-foot-square rooms, and an adjoining apartment for her younger daughter, Alice.

The move precipitated a simpler style that was more in keeping with the times, a change that was heralded in the hall by a strikingly contemporary console table from designer Nico Villeneuve. Elsewhere, Nina strikes a similar balance between classic and contemporary with dramatic touches such as a set of Hepplewhite dining chairs upholstered in fabric from the Philadelphia textile designers Liz Galbraith and Ephraim Paul and a graphic rug from The Rug Company. Architectural detail is kept to a minimum, as exemplified by the doorway that leads from the drawing room to the bedroom, which is devoid of decorative molding. The drawing room is dominated by a simple brass fireplace surround based on a design by Sir John Soane. There's an emphasis on mirrored surfaces; on one wall is a large collection of mirrored panels, and mirrored slips are set into the door surrounds. While the look is pared back compared to Nina's work up to that point, these crisp, contemporary details are balanced with dramatic curtains with swags and tails that are reminiscent of Nina's earlier work.

A console by designer Nico Villeneuve creates a striking welcome and distracts the eye from the inset radiator. A pair of bronze lion statuettes creates a balance between classic and contemporary and enhances the pleasing sense of symmetry.

The simple swag-and-tail curtains with contrasting lining are a nod to Nina's roots in classic decoration. The cushions on the sofa are in the striking Donuts fabric by Philadelphia-based studio Galbraith & Paul. In the foreground, the ever-faithful Archie commands the space.

ABOVE: The graphic work of art above the sofa in the living room makes a chic, contemporary statement. OPPOSITE: The fireplace surround, based on a design of Sir John Soane, was purchased at Jamb. Italian gilt oversized chairs were re-covered in a Pierre Frey satin stripe. The painting is by Sophie Coryndon. PAGE 190: In the dining room, a Biedermeier chest, surmounted by two Bianca Smith paintings, masks a hidden door. PAGE 191: The terrace, which can be accessed by French doors in the drawing room, the dining room, and the kitchen, has outdoor furniture from McKinnon and Harris.

The dining room is dominated by a large dresser, designed by Nina's friend
William Yeoward, which is glazed with mirror that allows it to blend into any space.
It appears again in Nina's next house (see pages 212–13). The Hepplewhite-style
chairs are in Galbraith & Paul's fabric Donuts, as are cushions in the drawing room.

In Nina's bedroom, a table designed by the Paris-based design partnership
R&Y Augousti, positioned in front of a window, lends the space a distinctive
Art Deco feel. The floor-to-ceiling bookshelves house a pair of radiators.

This apartment—like so many of Nina's residences—required clever use of space. A floor-to-ceiling wine storage unit (above) divides the kitchen from a dining area (opposite) that is accommodated in a conservatory-style extension. The latter is given a fresh look with blue-embellished monogrammed slipcovers, tableware, and glassware.

LONDON
CHELSEA

Nina's current home, which she affectionately calls "The Hut," is tucked away in one of South Kensington's many quiet backwaters, well away from the hustle and bustle of the Old Brompton Road. She tailored the house to her needs—raising the height of the roof and adding new windows to create a light, bright space for her bedroom suite on the top floor and excavating the basement to transform it into elegant, airy guest accommodation.

A sliding glass screen, decorated in an etched pattern reminiscent of fretwork panels by the Parisian designer Guillaume Saalburg, separates the drawing room from the dining room. When extended, it separates the two spaces, creating an intimate feel in the dining room. The drawing room is dominated by a simple, bolection-molding fireplace surround in a gilded finish that is set against a section of wall covered in mirrored glass. At one end is a hall-cum-library, and at the other, double doors lead to a small terrace. Like the larger terrace, which is accessed from the dining room, this area is lit at night to both create interest and extend the feeling of space. The ceilings are painted in a reflective lacquer that adds light and life to the interior.

In the entrance hall is a striking work of art, purchased from William Yeoward, that was previously in Nina's Notting Hill drawing room. Beneath it is a Lehmann bench from Nina Campbell Furniture that is upholstered in Boxwood from her collection for Osborne & Little.

The entrance hall doubles as a library that has the benefit of a skylight, which floods the space with diffuse natural light. In order to maximize light in the drawing room, the ceiling is painted in lacquer, creating a highly reflective finish. A screen creates a partial divide between the two spaces and provides a cozy backdrop for the armchair.

PRECEDING SPREAD AND
RIGHT: The drawing room is
furnished with armchairs
and a table from Nina
Campbell's furniture
collection. At night, outside
lights from the terrace help
to extend the feeling of
space. The gilded fireplace
surround was sourced by
Nina in Brooklyn.
FOLLOWING SPREAD:
Occasional furniture, small
fireside chairs, and quirky
decorative touches both
inherited and recently
acquired combine to create
a look that is comfortable
and highly personal.

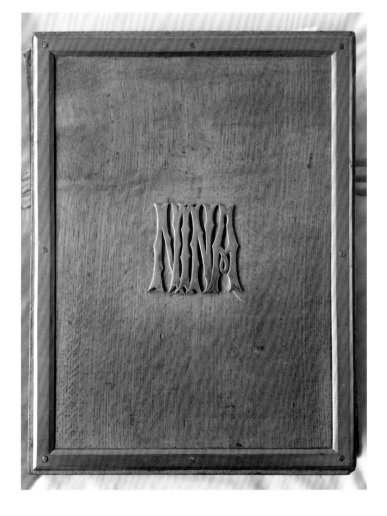

PRECEDING SPREAD: Much of the charm of The Hut is down to the eclectic mixed of old favorites and new acquisitions. They are set against a backdrop of Nina's fabrics and wallpapers. ABOVE: The decorative wall hanging (one of a pair) has appeared in the succession of residences that Nina has decorated since the early 1980s. OPPOSITE AND FOLLOWING SPREAD: The dining room can be separated from the drawing room with a sliding screen in etched glass by the Paris-based designer Guillaume Saalburg. The William Yeoward mirrored dresser, which was in Nina's previous residence, was altered to fit this new, smaller space.

PRECEDING PAGE: The discreetly hidden kitchen is fitted with shallow cabinets that make the most of the limited space. The window offers a view of a magnificent magnolia. ABOVE, OPPOSITE, AND FOLLOWING SPREAD: Nina's bedroom is a haven of comfort. Walls are upholstered in Nina's Penrose. Light from the wall of windows can be shielded with a plain pale-pink blind. The chair, upholstered in the same fabric as the walls, was part of the Nina Campbell Furniture collection. The headboard was custom-made in gray silk, outlined in two rows of nail heads. The mirror-glazed doors lead to the bathroom.

In the basement, the ground was excavated to lower the floor
and increase the ceiling height. The walls of the main
guest room (opposite) are covered in Nina's Barrington fabric.

NINA: A LONDON LIFE

With the exception of her time at school in Ascot and a few months in Paris, Nina has never lived anywhere but the Royal Borough of Kensington and Chelsea. It is where she was born, where she spent her childhood, where she built her thriving career, and where she brought up her children. Today it is a base for her travels all over the world—long trips to the United States and the Middle East overseeing projects and promoting her prolific work as a fabric and wallpaper designer. As the city has become ever more cosmopolitan, so has she. Now the designer is as at home in Brooklyn as she is in Bermuda, sometimes for pleasure but mostly for work. The result is a designer who is not only rooted in the heritage of the great city but also truly global in her outlook. Both influences have done much to enrich her contribution to interior design of the twentieth and twenty-first centuries.

The fourth-floor apartment on Sloane Street where Nina Campbell was born in May 1945 is on the fringes of Belgravia, the area where she was to spend her childhood in a succession of houses on the Grosvenor Estate. It is also on the same street where, seventeen years later, Nina started work at The General Trading Company, putting together wedding lists for engaged couples. Two miles north is Brook Street, where she was apprenticed to John Fowler (one half of Colefax and Fowler), a journey on which you'll pass Annabel's, the iconic London club she decorated for her friend Mark Birley. Less than half a mile west is 9 Walton Street, the shop where, for the last thirty years, Nina has created fabrics, wallpapers, and interior design schemes that offer her own colorful and comfortable interpretation of classic English style.

Two days before Nina's birth, German General Alfred Jodl signed a declaration of unconditional surrender in the French city of Reims. Belgravia, like the rest of London, had been ravaged by wartime bombing, yet postwar austerity did nothing to dampen the collective sense of relief that ensued. The houses where the young Campbell family lived were the setting for reeling parties and music recitals that heralded a new era. Nina's parents did not let shortages cramp their sense of style; Archie and Elizabeth Campbell shared a considerable flair for decorating that left each house in considerably better shape than they found them. It was no mean feat with resources in scarce supply.

The first residence that Nina can remember is 24 Lowndes Square, a house of palatial proportions. The sweeping staircase had steps covered in durable bottle-green art felt that was held in place with brass stair rods, meticulously polished every day—supplies were short, standards were not. It wasn't just the necessities that were scant (rationing didn't end until she was eleven); furnishings were, too. Nina remembers her mother buying a bolt of fabric that she dyed saffron yellow and used in the enormous drawing room with robin's-egg-blue walls. There followed a succession of houses in the area, which they never left. Nina's mother, who was Austrian, said that she "may be a refugee from Vienna but never from Belgravia." Nina attended school across the park in Bayswater, and her father worked for the magazine publisher Condé Nast. At eleven, Nina went to Heathfield School in Ascot, thirty miles west of London.

Nina's real education, however, came when she got her first job, at the age of seventeen. After spending time in Paris learning French, she worked for The General Trading Company, a quirky furnishings store that occupied two

OPPOSITE: Photographs from Nina's childhood in the late 1940s. With her parents, Colonel John Archibald Campbell and Elizabeth Pearth Campbell, she lived in a succession of houses in Belgravia and spent holidays in Scotland. ABOVE: Nina, photographed at the time she worked for Sibyl Colefax & John Fowler.

OPPOSITE: The interiors of Annabel's club in its first incarnation. The club's owner, Mark Birley, converted the Mayfair basement with the architect Philip Jebb and then enlisted Nina's help to work on the evolution of the original interiors. Together they collaborated on the interiors of Mark's Club and opened a shop near the Pimlico Road in Belgravia.
RIGHT: Mark Birley, in a Nina Campbell—decorated club room.

imposing houses on a corner of Sloane Square. With its china, glass, and furniture departments distributed between a chaotic arrangement of rooms, it offered a lighthearted antidote to the more staid option of neighboring department store Peter Jones.

The pivotal point in Nina's early career was being offered a job as an assistant by John Fowler of Colefax and Fowler. The business had been set up by Sibyl, Lady Colefax—the wife of patent lawyer Sir Arthur Colefax—who lost most of her fortune in the Wall Street market crash of 1929 and set up in business as an interior designer soon afterward.

Nina's years at Colefax and Fowler offered her an opportunity for complete immersion in every aspect of classic English decoration. The structure of the trade in the 1960s bore little relation to the glossy, high-rolling industry it became with the economic boom of the 1980s and the later influx of foreign investment in the London property market. Some of the finishing touches that elevated a Colefax interior above the ordinary—bullion fringes, tassels, silk lampshades—came as standard issue, so deep

knowledge was required to commission them from the cluster of artisanal businesses around Berners Street, Clerkenwell, and Shoreditch. Detail, clarity, and organization were as essential as design flair.

Although Nina was assigned to the office of Imogen Taylor, one of Colefax's most respected decorators, she also worked for other key figures in the firm, delivering bags to clients' houses for John Fowler and sourcing vivid linings for the suits of the chairman, Tom Parr. After three years, she left Colefax and set up on her own working for a variety of clients. It was during this period that she met Mark Birley, the entrepreneur who, in 1963, had opened Annabel's, a private members' nightclub in Berkeley Square.

The interiors at Annabel's had originally been created by Birley working in collaboration with the legendary Spanish interior decorator Jaime Parlade and the architect Philip Jebb. Birley employed Nina to work on the evolution of the interiors and, when he bought Siggy's, a restaurant on Charles Street, she did the interiors of Mark's Club from scratch. Unlike Annabel's, the new club offered

227

LEFT: Nina with her three children, Rita, Max, and Alice. OPPOSITE: The interiors of Chelsea Park Gardens, one of a succession of houses and apartments where Nina and her young family lived in Chelsea and South Kensington during the 1980s and 1990s. The decoration of her own residences offered an opportunity to experiment with new ideas. All were featured in magazines in the United Kingdom and abroad.

both lunch and dinner and was a refreshing alternative to the stuffier dining options of Claridge's, The Savoy, and Mirabel.

It was during this period that London began to shrug off the limitations of the postwar years and design became more progressive. But Nina and Mark Birley were less inspired by the new spirit of modernism that dominated the work of designers such as Robin Day or the spangly excesses of Biba than the effortless grandeur of the great European country houses of the late nineteenth century. Another project they worked on together was Nina Campbell & Mark Birley, a shop on the Pimlico Road near the Royal Hospital, Sir Christopher Wren's seventeenth-century masterpiece and home to the Chelsea Flower Show. At the time the area was London's answer to Paris's Left Bank—an important hub of antiques

dealers selling extravagant eighteenth-century furniture, presided over by Geoffrey Bennison, the antiques dealer turned decorator. Their shop sold luxuries such as Porthault bed linens and Fauchon sweets that would have been unimaginable a decade before.

Annabel's, Mark's Club, and the shop created a showcase for Nina's interior design abilities that brought a string of clients keen to enlist her talents. In 1973, she decided to go it alone and opened a shop at 48 and 54 Walton Street that served as both studio and store. The name "Nina Campbell" emblazoned above the door of a premises on this high-profile street—a stone's throw from the Victoria and Albert Museum, Harrods, and Hyde Park—also helped to establish the foundations for her meteoric rise. Thanks to deregulation of the stock market and burgeoning property prices, London was enjoying a

boom that did a huge amount to transform the interior design trade. Designers working on their own or in small partnerships were joined by practices with large teams working for wealthy clients and property developers. In turn, all this feverish activity stimulated the growth of businesses that serviced designers—fabric houses were transformed from cottage industries into household names while new magazines such as *The World of Interiors*, *Country Homes & Interiors*, and *Country Living* stimulated demand. Colefax and Fowler grew to include not just the original decorating business (known as Sibyl Colefax & John Fowler) but also brands such as Jane Churchill, Manuel Canovas, and Kingcome Sofas.

A flood of high-profile commissions followed, as did a growing collection of wallpapers and fabrics that were launched at the Decorex trade show, then held above Barkers department store on High Street Kensington. But it was two events in the late 1980s that transformed Nina from a sought-after London decorator to an international name. The first was a commission to design the interior of Sunninghill Park, the home of the newly married Duke and Duchess of York in Berkshire that generated publicity around the world. Commissions from Rod Stewart and Ringo Starr followed. The second was a manufacturing and distribution deal with the fabric and wallpaper brand Osborne & Little, owned

OPPOSITE: Nina with fabrics and wallpapers from her collections for Osborne & Little, the iconic British fabric and wallpaper brand established in 1968 by Sir Peter Osborne and his brother-in-law Anthony Little. For over thirty years, Nina has designed a succession of highly successful fabrics and wallpapers in partnership with the company that sell all over the world. ABOVE: Nina designed the plates and tablecloth fabric as part of her licensing lines.

by Sir Peter Osborne and Anthony Little. While so many designs at the time were slavish copies of eighteenth- and nineteenth-century originals, Nina used archival fabrics and wallpapers as the starting point for a design, playing with their scale as well as simplifying and re-coloring them to create motifs that were very much her own and that benefited her own experience as a decorator.

The demographic shift that was taking place in London's smarter postcodes during the 1980s meant that Nina's knack of manipulating space was a huge asset. London's growth as a financial center and cosmopolitan hub made it attractive to American financiers and the oil rich from the OPEC nations. The effect was to push a new generation of home-owners out of the palatial Belgravia and Mayfair town houses, which their parents had occupied, to flats, mews houses, and terraces farther west and

LEFT: A detail from Nina's bedroom at Drayton Gardens. OPPOSITE: In the late 1980s Nina's most high-profile commission was the decoration of Sunninghill Park in Ascot, which the Queen had given to the newly married Duke and Duchess of York as a wedding present. The project attracted significant press interest from all over the world, including *House & Garden* (US) magazine that featured a portrait of Nina by Lord Snowdon on its cover. FOLLOWING SPREAD: After Drayton Gardens, Nina moved to Chelsea Park Gardens, where, in her decoration of the drawing room, she created a simpler, more pared-back style, which came to dominate her work over the following decade.

to houses of more modest proportions in South Kensington and bohemian Chelsea. Nina's highly practical skills—her ability to create multifunctional rooms, to assemble space-saving but comfortable arrangements of furniture, and to find useful square footage on landings and beneath stairs—were essential as even the mega-wealthy had to scale back their living quarters.

The succession of houses that Nina bought, restored, and reconfigured mirrored the evolution of her life. In the late 1970s, the juggling act of simultaneously building a business while bringing up two small children—Rita, born in 1973, and Max, in 1976—was well served by an apartment on Drayton Gardens, just off the Fulham Road in Chelsea. Nina's decoration of the flat echoed the point that Annabel's demonstrated so eloquently a decade before—that you don't need palatial proportions to provide the comforts and elegance of an English country house. In the same way that they imbued a dark basement in Berkeley Square with the

rich, layered look of the Edwardian era, Nina employed all the techniques that she had learned with John Fowler, Imogen Taylor, and Mark Birley. In the drawing room, yellow Tisunique fabric on the walls finished with grosgrain ribbon and a deep red, gothic-style cornicing and a club fender created a comfortable but masculine feel.

The style was not derivative of the decorators Nina had worked with in her early career; instead, she forged her own distinctive look that became more pronounced with each new project. In the dining room of Drayton Gardens was a reinvention of the tradition, first inspired by Sir John Soane at his house in Lincoln's Inn, of painting dining rooms in a deep Pompeiian red. The habit not only related to classical revival but also conjured drama during the day and, at night, an intimate mood. Nina achieved these results with a deep cobalt blue that both gave a modern twist to a time-honored decorative tradition and, when combined with blue glass and pleated shades, created a cohesive, harmonious feel.

HG

HOUSE & GARDEN

MARCH 1989
$4.00

Nina Campbell,
Fergie's New Decorator

SPECIAL ISSUE
ENGLISH LIVING
AT ITS BEST

OPPOSITE: In 2007, Nina designed the interior of the Campbell Apartment, a cocktail lounge in a former Gilded Age private office in New York's Grand Central Terminal. RIGHT: Nina received the 2017 Design Leadership Award in San Francisco from the Design Leadership Network for her contribution to the professionalism and growth of the design industry.

Such bold statements were thanks to Nina's innate confidence, which allows her to manifest a distinctive style rather than schemes that slavishly mimic period looks. Nina's next move was to a house in Chelsea Park Gardens, a few streets away on the other side of the Fulham Road in an area known as the Little Boltons, which was dominated by large early Victorian double-fronted houses. In the first incarnation of the house during her ownership, the feel was simpler and more pared back. Here, the dining room was in dramatic—and much copied—cobalt blue, which carried through in the accessories on the dining table. Playful Gothic Revival touches were in evidence throughout the residence—in the delicate cornicing, the decorative screens, and joinery in the master bedroom.

Next stop was Harcourt Terrace, where paint effects in the entrance hall mimicked verdigris and trailing ivy, heralding a grand Empire style in the drawing room that achieved a masculine feel. Here, Nina's ability to create multifunctional spaces was demonstrated in the billiard table that doubled as a dining table. Everywhere, there were ideas that later became mainstream: broken pediments on joinery, glass doors backed with gathered fabric, and bold checks.

Meanwhile in her professional life, Nina's star was in the ascendant. The more high profile her commissions, the greater the attention of the press and she rapidly became a household name. Through the pages of magazines such as *House & Garden* and a number of books—as well as the lecture circuit on both sides of the Atlantic—Nina's ideas became highly influential. Her wit (that verges on stand-up comedy) and the generosity with which she shares her knowledge have made her a totemic figure for anyone interested in classic, comfortable interior design.

ACKNOWLEDGMENTS

Nina Campbell gratefully acknowledges the contributions of the following people:

My clients, without whom this book wouldn't be possible, for their support and friendship.

The wonderful Giles Kime, who has been instrumental in getting this book written and has also made it a dream to do.

Carolina Herrera for writing the foreword.

Philip Reeser, my editor at Rizzoli, for his enormous patience and humor throughout, even when thrown a change of mind at the eleventh hour.

Charles Miers, my publisher at Rizzoli, and Doug Turshen and Steve Turner, who so elegantly designed this book.

Paul Raeside for his good humor, hard work, and beautiful photography.

Alice Deen for coordinating everything for us from start to delivery of the book.

Georg Lauth and my interior design team as well as all the unsung heroes of the entire Nina Campbell team and beyond—none of this would happen without all of their hard work and dedication.

John Carter and his team for delivering incredible flowers, always being so positive and creative, and making everything a possibility.

The Garvey Brothers, Len Carter, Henry van der Vyver, and all the people we work with on a daily basis for their endless support on all projects.

Eliot Wright and Jim Sersich from Partners in Design; Dean Barger; Kate Brodsky of KRB; and Scott Sottile and the Ferguson & Shamamian team for all their help in the United States.

Joshua McHugh, Simon Brown, and Bethany Nauert for their photography.

Dasha Epstein for her friendship and endless generosity in providing me with a home away from home in New York City.

My children, grandchildren, family, and friends for their endless love, support, and understanding.

I would like to dedicate this book to the antiques dealers I visit and to all the craftsmen who make our work possible.

This book would never have have seen the light of day without an impromptu cup of tea at The Capital Hotel in Knightsbridge, the brilliance and wit of Nina Campbell (whose openness and generosity of spirit magically make things happen), the patience and wisdom of Philip Reeser, or the persistence and determination of Alice Deen. —*Giles Kime*

PHOTOGRAPHY CREDITS

Paul Raeside: 2, 6, 29, 30–31, 32, 33, 34, 35, 36, 37, 38, 39, 40, 41, 42, 43, 44, 45, 46, 47, 48, 50, 51, 52, 53, 54–55, 56, 57, 58, 58–59, 60–61, 62, 63, 64, 65, 66–67, 68, 69, 70, 71, 72–73, 74, 75, 76, 77, 100, 102–03, 104, 105, 106, 107, 108, 109, 110–11, 112–13, 114, 115, 116–17, 118, 119, 120–21, 123, 124–25, 126, 127, 128, 129, 131, 133, 134, 135, 136, 136–37, 138, 139, 140, 141, 142–43, 144, 145, 146–47, 148, 149, 150–51, 152, 153, 154, 155, 156, 157, 202–03, 208 (top right), 209 (bottom right), 212–13, 215, 218–19, 220, 221, 239

Joshua McHugh: 4, 12, 14–15, 16–17, 18, 19, 20, 21, 22, 23, 24, 25, 26, 27

Simon Brown: 79, 80–81, 82–83, 84–85, 86, 87, 88–89, 90–91, 92, 93, 94, 95, 96, 97, 98–99, 198, 200–01, 204–05, 206, 207, 208 (top left, bottom right, bottom left), 209 (top left, top right, bottom left), 210, 211, 214, 216, 217

James Davidson: 130

Bethany Nauert: 158, 160–61, 162–63, 164, 165, 166–67, 168, 169

James Mortimer / *House & Garden*: 173, 174, 175, 176–77 178–79, 180–81, 182, 183

Andreas Von Einsiedel / *House & Garden* © The Condé Nast Publications Ltd.: 184, 190, 193, 194, 195, 196, 197

Photography by Jan Baldwin © CICO Books: 186–87, 188, 189, 191, 192

Collection of Nina Campbell: 224, 225, 229, 230

Mirrorpix / Getty Images: 227

Lucinda Lambton: 228

Fritz von der Schulenburg / The Interior Archive: 226, 231, 234 (bottom left), 235 (top right)

Christopher Simon Sykes / The Interior Archive: 232, 234 (top and bottom right), 235 (top left and bottom)

Antony Armstrong-Jones / *House & Garden* © Condé Nast: 233

Photograph by Benjamin Hill. Copyright © Hospitality Holdings, Inc. / The Campbell Apartment: 236

Simon Chu: 237

Fabrics by Nina Campbell, distributed by Osborne & Little

Photography courtesy of Osborne & Little

Front endpapers: Loulou in Indigo and La Moulade in Indigo/Crimson

Page 10: Barrington in Pale Blue

Page 11: Bicton in Pale Steel Blue

Page 170: Camille in Grey/Beige

Page 171: Meredith in Beige

Page 222: Keightley's Folio in Sepia

Page 223: Pampelonne in Beige

Back endpapers: Birdcage Walk in Cream/Blue and Beau Rivage in Blue/Indigo

First published in the United States of America in 2018 by
Rizzoli International Publications, Inc.
300 Park Avenue South
New York, NY 10010
www.rizzoliusa.com

Copyright © 2018 by Nina Campbell
Text: Copyright © 2018 by Giles Kime
ISBN: 978-0-8478-6317-4
Library of Congress Control Number: 2018938666

For Rizzoli International Publications:
Philip Reeser, Editor
Alyn Evans, Production Manager
Elizabeth Smith, Copy Editor

Design: Doug Turshen with Steve Turner
Printed in China
2018 2019 2020 2021 / 10 9 8 7 6 5 4 3 2 1